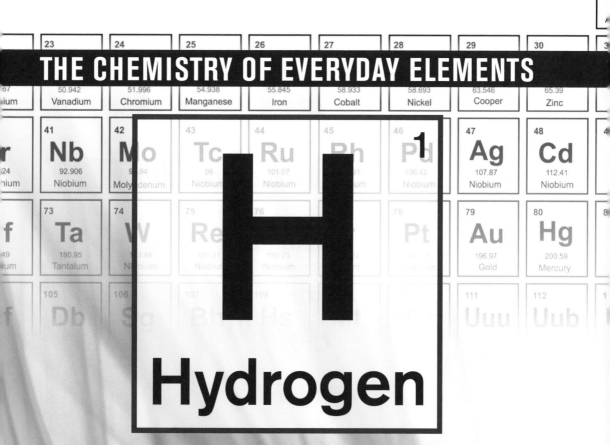

THE CHEMISTRY OF EVERYDAY ELEMENTS

23	24	25	26	27	28	29	30
50.942	51.996	54.938	55.845	58.933	58.693	63.546	65.39
Vanadium	Chromium	Manganese	Iron	Cobalt	Nickel	Cooper	Zinc

41	42	43	44	45	46		47	48
Nb	**Mo**	Tc	Ru	Rh	Pd	**1**	**Ag**	**Cd**
92.906	95.94	98	101.07	91	106.42		107.87	112.41
Niobium	Molybdenum	Niobium	Niobium	ium	Niobium		Niobium	Niobium

H
Hydrogen

73	74	75	76		78	79	80
Ta	W	Re			Pt	**Au**	**Hg**
180.95	183.84	186.21	190.23			196.97	200.59
Tantalum	Niobium	Niobium	Niobium			Gold	Mercury

105	106	107	108	111	112
Db	Sg	Bh	Hs	Uuu	Uub

Mason Crest

1

THE CHEMISTRY OF EVERYDAY ELEMENTS

Aluminum

Carbon

Gold

Helium

Hydrogen

Oxygen

Silicon

Silver

Understanding the Periodic Table

Uranium

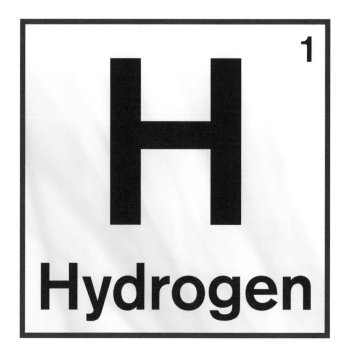

H 1
Hydrogen

By Kathryn Hulick

Mason Crest
450 Parkway Drive, Suite D
Broomall, PA 19008
www.masoncrest.com

Printed and bound in the United States of America.

Series ISBN: 978-1-4222-3837-0
Hardback ISBN: 978-1-4222-3842-4
EBook ISBN: 978-1-4222-7947-2

First printing
1 3 5 7 9 8 6 4 2

Produced by Shoreline Publishing Group LLC
Santa Barbara, California
Editorial Director: James Buckley Jr.
Designer: Patty Kelley
www.shorelinepublishing.com

Library of Congress Cataloging-in-Publication Data on file with the Publisher.

Cover photographs by Dreamstime.com: Warren Rosenberg (car); Michelle Meiklejohn (corn). Department of Defense (explosion).

QR Codes disclaimer:

Hydrogen

Introduction **6**

Discovery and History **12**

Chemical Properties **22**

Hydrogen and You **30**

Hydrogen Combines **34**

Hydrogen in Our World **44**

Find Out More **62**

Series Glossary of Key Terms **63**

Index/Author **64**

KEY ICONS TO LOOK FOR

Words to Understand: These words with their easy-to-understand definitions will increase the reader's understanding of the text, while building vocabulary skills.

Sidebars: This boxed material within the main text allows readers to build knowledge, gain insights, explore possibilities, and broaden their perspectives by weaving together additional information to provide realistic and holistic perspectives.

Educational Videos: Readers can view videos by scanning our QR codes, providing them with additional educational content to supplement the text. Examples include news coverage, moments in history, speeches, iconic moments, and much more!

Text-Dependent Questions: These questions send the reader back to the text for more careful attention to the evidence presented here.

Research Projects: Readers are pointed toward areas of further inquiry connected to each chapter. Suggestions are provided for projects that encourage deeper research and analysis.

Series Glossary of Key Terms: This back-of-the-book glossary contains terminology used throughout this series. Words found here increase the reader's ability to read and comprehend higher-level books and articles in this field.

Introduction

Look around. What do you see? Maybe a cell phone, a half-eaten banana, and a glass of water sit on the table. Outside your window, you might see clouds or rain or the sun shining. What do you feel? Your breath travels in and out, filling your lungs, while your heart pumps

---

WORDS TO UNDERSTAND

DNA deoxyribonucleic acid; a material inside the cells of most living organisms that carries genetic information

hydrogen fuel cell a battery-like device in which hydrogen fuels a chemical reaction that produces electricity

isotope an atom of a specific element that has a different number of neutrons; it has the same atomic number but a different atomic mass

---

blood around your body. All of those things—the solids, liquids, and gases around you and inside you—are composed of elements of the periodic table.

Hydrogen and its one proton form the simplest elemental structure.

The periodic table is an arrangement of all the naturally occurring, and manufactured, elements known to humans at this point in time. An element is a substance that cannot be broken down into other elements. Ninety-two elements occur naturally on Earth and in space. Twenty-six more elements (and counting) have been manufactured and analyzed in a laboratory setting. These elements, alone or in combination with others, form and shape all the matter around us. From the air we breathe, to the water we drink, to the bananas we eat—all these things are made of elements.

These elements are organized into a chart called the periodic table. Since it was first developed in 1869, the periodic table went through several updates and reorganizations until it became the modern version of the table used today. On it, each square represents a single ele-

Hydrogen

ment. These elements are arranged into rows and columns by increasing atomic number. The atomic number equals the number of protons in the nucleus of the atom. Each element has a unique atomic number. Oxygen has an atomic number of 8 because it has eight protons in its nucleus. The nucleus of an atom may also contain neutrons. When an atom has the same number of protons as an element on the chart, but a different number of neutrons, it is called an **isotope**.

Each element on the periodic table has its own unique chemical and physical properties. The chart helps keep track of elements with certain properties by arranging them into columns, groups, or rows. In addition to the atomic number, each square in the periodic table also lists the name of the element and its abbreviation (H for hydrogen), along with other important information such as the number of neutrons in the nucleus of one atom of an element, the number of electrons that surround the nucleus, the atomic mass, and the general size of the atom. The periodic table is a very useful tool as one begins to investigate chemistry and science in general. (For lots more on the periodic table, read *Understanding the Periodic Table*, another book in this series.)

This book is about the element hydrogen. Hydrogen is element number 1 on the periodic table, and is the most abundant element in

Periodic Table

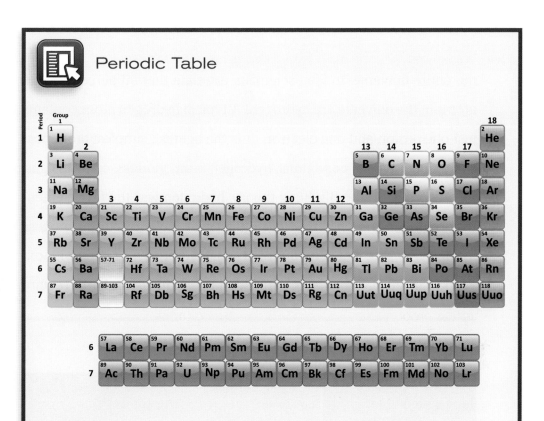

The Periodic Table of the Elements is arranged in numerical order. The number of each element is determined by the number of protons in its nucleus. The horizontal rows are called periods. The number of the elements increases across a period, from left to right. The vertical columns are called groups. Groups of elements share similar characteristics. The colors, which can vary depending on the way the creators design their version of the chart, also create related collections of elements, such as noble gases, metals, or nonmetals, among others.

the entire universe. In fact, scientists estimate that 90 percent of the atoms in the universe are hydrogen! A typical hydrogen atom contains just one proton and one electron. It is the lightest, simplest atom possible. Under typical conditions, hydrogen is an odorless, colorless gas.

According to the Big Bang theory, hydrogen was the first element to form when the universe began. Today, it fuels the fusion process inside every star, including our own sun. Hydrogen also joins with oxygen to make H_2O, or water. Almost all living things on Earth require

The power of hydrogen sent the NASA Space Shuttles into outer space.

energy from the sun and water to survive. Without hydrogen, life as we know it could not exist.

Beyond helping to provide life, hydrogen is a key part making that life more livable. Hydrogen is an important component of plastic, gasoline, and fertilizer. It holds **DNA** and most other molecules in living cells together. Hydrogen can also provide energy. Liquid hydrogen propels rockets into space. Natural gas, a very important fuel for heating, power plants, and more, contains hydrogen bonded with carbon to form a gas called methane.

A **hydrogen fuel cell** is a battery-like device. It could help power electric cars, taking the place of an internal combustion engine. These fuel cell cars emit only water vapor in place of toxic, smelly exhaust. Hydrogen could also store energy for later use. Extra electricity from power plants or renewable energy sources could go towards producing hydrogen, which could then be converted back into electricity in a fuel cell. Many believe that hydrogen is the fuel of the future.

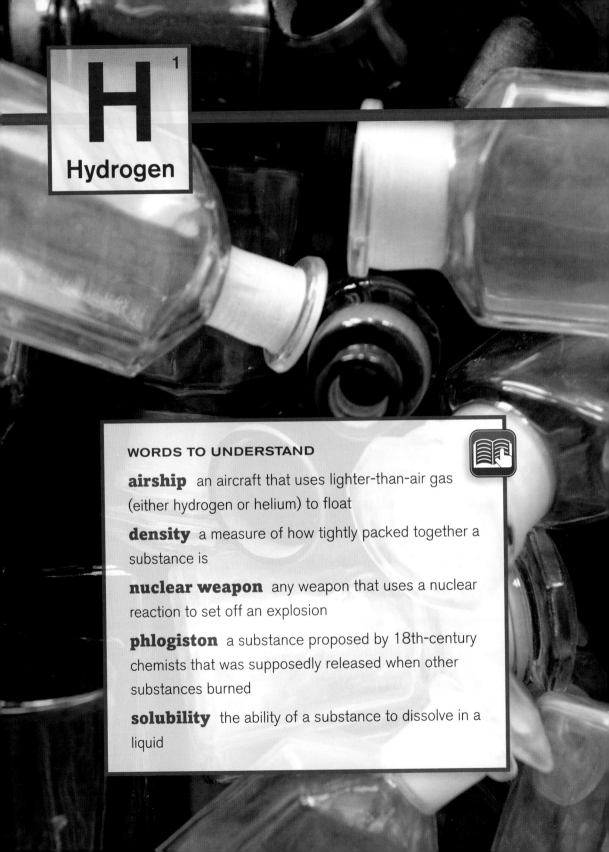

H ¹

Hydrogen

WORDS TO UNDERSTAND

airship an aircraft that uses lighter-than-air gas (either hydrogen or helium) to float

density a measure of how tightly packed together a substance is

nuclear weapon any weapon that uses a nuclear reaction to set off an explosion

phlogiston a substance proposed by 18th-century chemists that was supposedly released when other substances burned

solubility the ability of a substance to dissolve in a liquid

Discovery and History

Philosophers in ancient Greece theorized that everything in the world was made up of just four elements: earth, air, fire, and water. This theory persisted into the 18th century, when chemists in England and France finally proved that water and air could be broken down into several different elements, one of which, of course, was hydrogen. Hydrogen got its name from the Greek words, *hydro* (water) and *genes* (generator), because hydrogen forms water.

Air on Fire

Long before hydrogen got its name and place on the periodic table, scientists and alchemists had noted its existence. They had performed experiments that gave off hydrogen gas.

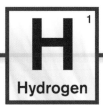

H ¹

Hydrogen

However, at the time, these experimenters did not recognize that the gas they had produced was a separate element. They usually thought it was just another form of air.

In one example of such an experiment from 1671, Robert Boyle, an English chemist, added iron to two different acids—hydrochloric acid (HCl) and sulfuric acid (H_2SO_4). Both reactions gave off a gas that easily caught on fire. Boyle referred to this gas as an "inflammable solution of Mars," where "Mars" refers to the iron and "inflammable" means "easy to set on fire."

Thanks to a large inheritance, British scientist Henry Cavendish could spend all his time in a lab.

However, Henry Cavendish is the one usually credited with the discovery of hydrogen. Cavendish, a shy, eccentric English chemist, avoided social functions and close relationships. Though he had inherited a huge fortune, he spent almost all his time alone in his lab. In 1766, he repeated Boyle's experiment with sulfuric acid, and produced hydrogen, which he called "inflammable air." He took the experiment to the next level when he isolated the gas inside a bottle. He also measured several important properties of the gas, including its **solubility** in water and its **density**.

In 1783, Cavendish performed another experiment with his "inflammable air." He discovered that burning hydrogen with oxygen produces water. This is not at all the result he expected. First of all, many people still thought water was a basic element that couldn't be created by combining other things. Secondly, he adhered to a popular theory at the time involving a theoretical substance found in fire called **phlogiston**. He thought his "inflammable air" was pure phlogiston.

If not for another chemist, Frenchman Antoine Lavoisier, we might speak today about *phlogistating* with water instead of *hydrating* with water. Often called the father of modern chemistry, Lavoisier

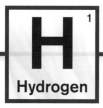
 Phlogiston

Phlogiston chemistry may be wrong, but it was an interesting theory, originally developed by German scientist Georg Ernst Stahl in the early 18th century. The theory held that everything combustible contains a substance called "phlogiston." When a thing burns, phlogiston escapes into the air. Phlogiston comes from a Greek word that means "inflammable," or easy to set on fire.

Georg Erneſtus Stahl, Onoldo Francus,
Med. Doct. h.t. Prof. Publ. Ord. Hall.

Georg Ernst Stahl

By the mid-18th century, when Henry Cavendish was experimenting with gases, chemists had decided that nitrogen was phlogistated air and oxygen was dephlogistated air. Cavendish theorized that hydrogen was pure phlogiston. Therefore, he figured that adding phlogiston to dephlogistated air would give him phlogistated air. In other words, he thought hydrogen plus oxygen would equal nitrogen. Of course that's not true at all. Instead, the reaction forms water. Phlogiston chemistry was doomed to failure.

did away with phlogiston chemistry and the old Greek notion of four elements, too. He is perhaps best known for his discovery of oxygen in 1778. But he also repeated Cavendish's water experiment later in 1783, and correctly deduced that oxygen had combined with the "inflammable air" to produce water. He gave "inflammable air" the name "hydrogen," or "water-forming."

Balloons, Blimps, and Zeppelins

In 1783, the same year that Cavendish and Lavoisier were figuring out hydrogen's properties, engineers were already putting the element to use. Hydrogen gas is much lighter than air, meaning that enough of the gas can make an aircraft fly.

The first hydrogen balloon took flight in August 1783 from the site in France where the Eiffel Tower now stands. To get enough hydrogen to lift the balloon, its builders poured about a quarter ton of sulfuric acid over a half ton of iron. The balloon traveled 13 miles (20.9 km), then landed in a remote village. The terrified people there promptly attacked the strange "UFO" with pitchforks and knives!

Early hydrogen balloons could not speed up, slow down, or steer.

They simply floated with the wind. In time, however, **airships** would rival airplanes for dominion over the skies. In 1852, the first dirigible, a hydrogen-filled airship, launched from Paris. This craft could be steered with a steam-powered propeller and a rudder. However, the most famous airship of all arrived in 1900: the zeppelin. Count Ferdinand von Zeppelin devoted much of his life to developing new and better zeppelins.

During a test of an early zeppelin in 1908, the ship crashed and then exploded in a fireball. The problem? Hydrogen. While hydrogen's lighter-than-air property makes it great at lifting, it has another, more dangerous property. Remember that early name, "inflammable air"? Hydrogen burns very easily with an extremely

Airships like these were once seen as airplane substitutes.

hot flame. All it takes is some oxygen and a little spark to set off a powerful explosion. Helium, the second-lightest element on the periodic table, does not explode. Some early airships used helium, but this element is rare and more difficult to obtain than hydrogen.

The *Hindenburg* disaster

Despite the danger, airship travel seemed to be the future. By the 1930s, luxurious airships regularly carried passengers between Europe and North or South America. But that all ended in 1937, with the explosion of the *Hindenburg*. The ship was about to dock in New Jersey after a flight from Germany when it burst into flames, then crashed. An accidental burst of static electricity likely ignited the hydrogen gas. Thirty-six people died, and the disaster was caught on camera. Today's blimps are filled with helium.

The *Hindenburg* explosion was not the first, or even the most deadly, disaster in airship history. But it caused the general public to lose faith in the technology and brought an end to the era of the airship. However, the history of hydrogen's explosive power was far from over.

H 1

Hydrogen

Bombs Away

World War II prompted the development of **nuclear weapons**. Atomic bombs rely on radioactive elements, typically isotopes of uranium or plutonium. When these elements break apart in a chain reaction, they release huge amounts of energy. Near the end of World War II, the United States destroyed two cities in Japan with atomic bombs, killing more than 200,000 civilians. Even after the war, the United States and the Soviet Union kept trying to build even bigger bombs.

In 1952, the U.S. set off the world's first thermonuclear weapon, a hydrogen bomb, or H-bomb, on an island in the Pacific Ocean. It was just a test. The very next year, the Soviet Union also tested the same kind of bomb. Many people feared that these tests might lead to a world-ending war. A regular atomic bomb sits at the heart of an H-bomb. A single H-bomb could destroy a large city.

Scientists who understood the potential of such a bomb tried to stop its construction. The General Advisory Committee to the U.S. Atomic Energy Commission published a report regarding construction of an H-bomb in 1949. In one section of the report, physicists Enrico Fermi and Isidor Rabi wrote, "The fact that no limits exist to the destructiveness of this weapon makes its very existence and the knowledge of its construction a danger to humanity as a whole. It is necessarily an evil thing considered in any light."

Despite Fermi and Rabi's misgivings, the hydrogen bomb was built. However, the same fusion reaction that is so devastating in a bomb also has the potential to generate huge amounts of electricity. See more about fusion reactors in Chapter 4. Scientists still have a long way to go before fusion can become a reliable source of power.

 Text-Dependent Questions

1. What is phlogiston?

2. What makes hydrogen a dangerous choice for filling airships?

3. What happened to the *Hindenburg*?

Research Project

Make a chart comparing the potential risk of nuclear warfare to the potential benefit of fusion power. Do you think it's better for people to have both technologies or neither?

H ¹

Hydrogen

WORDS TO UNDERSTAND

covalent bond a bond in which electron pairs are shared between atoms

hydrogen bond a weak bond in which a hydrogen atom in one molecule is attracted to an atom in another molecule

ion an atom or molecule that has lost or gained electrons, and thus has either a positive or negative electric charge

Chemical Properties

Hydrogen is like the secret agent of the elements. In gas form, hydrogen is completely invisible and has no scent or taste. Plus, it's the smallest atom possible. It's lighter than air and can easily escape containment. One way to detect hydrogen is to light a small sample on fire. Hydrogen is extremely flammable and burns up very quickly when exposed to air and a spark. This is called the "pop" test because the tiny explosion of a small amount of hydrogen makes a "pop" sound.

Bonding

Every atom is composed of a nucleus surrounded by electrons. These electrons organize themselves into levels, known

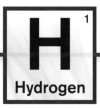

Hydrogen

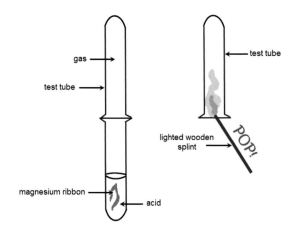

gas →

test tube →

← test tube

lighted wooden splint →

POP!

magnesium ribbon →

← acid

This experiment shows the "pop" test to demonstrate the presence of hydrogen.

as orbitals, or shells. Each shell has an ideal number of electrons. When that number is reached, the atom becomes stable. Hydrogen has just one electron in the very first orbital. But that shell needs two electrons for stability. To achieve stability, atoms can share their electrons. All hydrogen gas is actually made up of pairs of bonded hydrogen atoms, known as H_2. Each pair shares two electrons.

But hydrogen doesn't always bond with itself. It can also bond with pretty much anything else that needs an electron to fill its outer most orbital. Sometimes, these relationships result in an even sharing of electrons, called a **covalent** (koh-VALE-ent) **bond**. Other times, the relationship is unequal. Hydrogen is a tiny atom, and its electron may spend more time hanging around the larger atom. So the larger atom becomes negatively charged and the hydrogen becomes positively

Hydrogen Isotopes

Hydrogen has three isotopes: hydrogen itself, plus deuterium and tritium. The second two are the only two to have their own names. Other isotopes have a name such as "carbon-14"— the name of the base element, plus the number of neutrons in the nucleus of the isotope. The nucleus of a normal hydrogen atom contains one proton and zero neutrons. Deuterium contains one neutron in addition to the proton, and tritium contains two neutrons and a proton.

The discovery of deuterium in 1932 earned American chemist Harold C. Urey the Nobel Prize in chemistry. Radioactive tritium was discovered two years later, in 1934. Deuterium weighs twice as much as hydrogen, but it can still form water. Water with a high concentration of D_2O molecules is called "heavy water." Deuterium, tritium, and heavy water can all be used in nuclear reactors or to produce nuclear weapons, so these substances are tightly controlled. For example, the radioactivity of tritium can produce a glowing light that's not dangerous and looks cool in watches and keychains. But the U.S. Nuclear Regulatory Commission blocks the sale of some of these products in the U.S.

Hydrogen

charged. These charges attract, and keep the atoms together. This type of bond is so important that it has its own name: a **hydrogen bond**. This kind of bond joins water molecules together; a droplet on a leaf holds its shape due to hydrogen bonds. These bonds also join together the molecules that make up living cells, proteins, and DNA.

Double Agent

Though most periodic tables place hydrogen at the top of the left-most column, it doesn't really belong there. All the rest of the elements in that column are soft metals at room temperature, while hydrogen is a gas. But sometimes, hydrogen does act like a metal. This element really belongs in its own, special category. Hydrogen isn't just any secret agent — it's a double agent!

Hydrogen is very light, does not conduct electricity, and is a gas at room temperature. It also tends to form negative ions, called hydrides, in chemical reactions. So it seems like a nonmetal. However, hydrogen may also lose its single electron to form a positive **ion**. This happens when acids dissolve in water. In addition, hydrogen becomes even more like a metal in its liquid and solid states.

At very low temperatures or extreme pressures, hydrogen will transform into a liquid or a solid. The center of the planet Jupiter is most likely liquid hydrogen. In *NASA Science News*, NASA scientist Scott Bolton said, "Here on Earth, hydrogen is a colorless, transparent gas," he said. "But in the core of Jupiter, hydrogen transforms into something bizarre." This liquid hydrogen reflects light like a mirror

 Metal vs. Nonmetal

Here are some of the differences between metals and nonmetals:

	Metals	Nonmetals
appearance	shiny	dull
state	solid at room temperature (except for mercury)	solid, liquid, or gas at room temperature
density	high (heavy)	low (light)
ability to conduct electricity	good	poor
behavior in a chemical reaction	lose electrons easily to form positive ions	gain electrons easily to form negative ions

Hydrogen

and conducts electricity, both properties typical of metals.

Jupiter may also contain solid metallic hydrogen, and researchers are close to producing this strange substance on Earth. They have used diamonds to generate extreme pressures, squashing hydrogen until the bonds between its molecules shift. A 2017 report said some scientists had done it, but others questioned their methods.

Transporting Hydrogen

Hydrogen gas escapes through even the tiniest hole. For these reasons, hydrogen is often transported in liquid form. Liquid hydrogen is hard to handle. It must be compressed and cooled to a frigid −423 degrees°F (−253°C). It takes a lot of energy to maintain the low temperature and high pressure required to keep hydrogen in a liquid form. But the effort pays off, especially if you're an astronaut or rocket scientist. Liquid hydrogen is the fuel of choice for spacecraft. NASA needed to develop many safeguards to safely handle liquid hydrogen. The fuel travels to a spacecraft through pipelines. A leak in a pipe can spew invisible hydrogen gas into the air, which could lead to a deadly inferno. Remember the *Hindenburg* disaster? A group of researchers set out to develop a tape that would change color quickly when exposed to hydrogen gas. NASA used this tape to successfully detect and pinpoint the source of a leak in 2007. The tape could also be useful in other industries.

Liquid hydrogen rocket

 Text-Dependent Questions

1. What are two different ways that you could detect hydrogen gas?

2. Why does hydrogen form bond with other atoms?

3. Why is hydrogen's correct placement on the periodic table unclear?

Research Project

Look for recent news on metallic hydrogen research. What are scientists doing to try to create this material? What do they think it could be used for? Write a paragraph about the current state of this research, including predictions about whether or not you think metallic hydrogen will ever be manufactured and used in the real world.

Hydrogen and You

Life cannot exist without hydrogen. First of all, hydrogen powers the sun, which provides the energy all living things need to survive. Plants take in energy directly from the sun in order to perform photosynthesis. Then animals recycle that energy by eating the plants (or each other).

Secondly, hydrogen puts the H in H_2O, and water is essential to life. Water vapor on Earth helps trap sunlight, keeping the climate warm. Without water vapor in the atmosphere, Earth may have remained too cold to support life. Liquid water

WORDS TO UNDERSTAND

carbohydrates a group of organic compounds including sugars, starches, and fiber

saturated fat a fat derived from animal products that is solid at room temperature

unsaturated fat a fat derived from plants and some animals that is liquid at room temperature

in the oceans also helps to keep Earth's temperature in a comfortable range. In fact, in the search for life on other planets, scientists look for the presence of liquid water.

You could survive for several weeks without eating, but most people would last just a few days without any water. A little more than half of your body weight is water. What does all that water do for you? Sweat helps regulate your body temperature, and urine carries toxic substances out of the body. Water also acts as a shock absorber to protect the brain and spine, it forms saliva, and it helps your joints move smoothly. Less than one percent of the water in your body ends up involved in a chemical reaction, but these reactions are very important. Water helps break down proteins and sugars in the food you eat into smaller pieces that your body can use for energy.

Most of the food you eat also contains hydrogen inside of molecules known as **carbohydrates**. These molecules combine carbon, hydrogen, and oxygen. The three main types of carbohydrates are sugars, starches, and fiber. Foods rich in carbohydrates include bread, pasta, rice, potatoes, candy, chips, crackers, fruit, and milk.

Though many fad diets blame "carbs" for making people fat, the truth is that you need carbohydrates to survive. You might get fat, though, if you eat too many of the wrong kind of carbohydrates and don't get enough exercise. Healthy carbohydrates, such as whole grains, fruits, and beans, take longer for the body to process. Unhealthy carbohydrates supply quick energy. Examples include foods and drinks with added sugar or refined grains, such as sweetened drinks, white bread, and white rice.

What's in Your Peanut Butter?

Hydrogen is found in in healthy and unhealthy fats, too. If you happen to have a jar of peanut butter nearby, take a look at the ingredients. Unless you happen to buy natural peanut butter, you'll see some sort of "hydrogenated oil" on the list. That means oil that has had hydrogen added to it.

Oil is a kind of fat, and all fats contain carbon and hydrogen, linked together into a chain called a hydrocarbon. In some of these chains, every carbon atom is linked to the maximum number of hydrogen atoms. This is called a **saturated fat**, because it is full of hydrogen—it can't hold any more. In an **unsaturated fat**, there are gaps in the chain where hydrogen atoms are missing.

Unsaturated fats can be found in foods including vegetable oils, nuts, avocados, and soybeans. Saturated fats are commonly found in meat, butter, ice cream, and other animal products. Saturated fats increase levels of bad cholesterol in the body, a condition that can lead to heart disease. Unsaturated fat helps reduce bad cholesterol and raise good cholesterol.

A third kind of fat exists, one that people created: trans fat. Food manufacturers figured out that adding some hydrogen to unsaturated, liquid fats would make them more solid. Margarine is an ex-

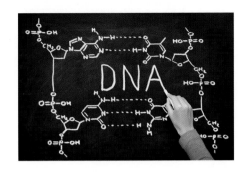

ample of a partially hydrogenated vegetable oil. The chemical structure of a trans fat falls somewhere in between saturated and unsaturated.

Eventually researchers learned that trans fats are very unhealthy. They increase bad cholesterol and decrease good cholesterol. So, fewer foods contain trans fats. However, you may still find them in fried foods, doughnuts, cookies, and crackers. Look for "partially hydrogenated" oil on the ingredients list.

But don't blame hydrogen for the unhealthiness of some carbohydrates and some fats. Remember, hydrogen is there in healthy foods, too. And it's also an essential ingredient of good old H_2O. It's safe to say that hydrogen is an important part of a healthy diet.

Also, the coiling double-helix structure of DNA, which forms all our cells, wouldn't be possible without hydrogen bonds. These bonds join together the bases, or building blocks, of DNA into pairs.

H ¹

Hydrogen

WORDS TO UNDERSTAND

acid a substance that forms hydrogen ions when dissolved in water, typically corrosive or sour-tasting

hydrocarbon a compound formed from hydrogen and carbon atoms

nebula a massive cloud of gas and dust in outer space

pH a measurement of how acidic or alkaline (basic) a solution is

Hydrogen Combines

Hydrogen combines with pretty much anything and everything. Millions of chemical compounds contain hydrogen, from water to sugar, vinegar, baking soda, plastic, and gasoline. When atoms combine with each other, they either share or transfer their electrons. Remember that a stable atom is one with a full outer shell of electrons. A single hydrogen atom has just one electron, but needs two in its shell in order to be stable. However, hydrogen doesn't just share an electron. It will also give up its single electron. Since it can gain or lose an electron, hydrogen easily combines with many, many other atoms.

Water, Water Everywhere

Hydrogen is the third most abundant element on Earth, after oxygen and silicon. Most of the hydrogen on Earth is found

Hydrogen

in water, or H_2O. Even though hydrogen is the lightest element of all, it makes up about 10 percent of the mass of Earth's oceans.

The water on Earth originally formed in outer space, and was likely delivered to our planet when asteroids or comets crashed into the surface. Water is actually quite common in the universe, though it's usually not liquid–it's either a gas called water vapor, or frozen solid as ice.

In areas of the universe where stars are being born, hydrogen may combine with oxygen to make water vapor. Astronomers have observed this process happening in the Orion **Nebula**. "In all the sky that we've observed, that's the strongest source of water," said Gary Melnick of Harvard University in an interview with the author. The Orion Nebula generates enough water to fill up Earth's oceans every 24 minutes.

Water vapor also forms slowly in cold clouds of gas. Similarly, ice may form very slowly on tiny dust grains. All it takes is an oxygen atom randomly colliding with some hydrogen atoms. Over long periods of time, these random encounters may happen often enough for vapor or ice to build up.

Three forms of water—vapor, solid ice, and liquid—all together in one glass.

The Magical Liquid

Water is a very special chemical compound. In addition to being essential for human and animal life, it has some unusual properties. When an element solidifies, it usually becomes denser and heavier. Yet when water freezes into ice, it expands. Ice is lighter than water, not heavier, which is why ice cubes and icebergs float. This happens because the hydrogen bonds between molecules of H_2O form a solid with a very open crystal structure.

Water is also an excellent solvent, meaning that many other materials easily dissolve in water. For example, if you sprinkle salt into water, the solid grains of salt gradually dissolve into the liquid. The same thing happens if you drop in a sugar cube, a scoop of instant coffee, or some powdered laundry detergent. Water dissolves more substances than any other liquid.

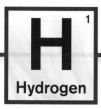

Hydrogen

 Acid Rain

When factories, power plants, and cars release pollution into the air, some of these gases react with the water in clouds to form sulphuric and nitric **acid**. When the clouds release the polluted droplets, we call it acid precipitation. The term sounds scary, but it won't burn your skin if you happen to get caught in an acid rain shower. The acid simply isn't strong enough. However, it can still harm the environment. If enough acid rain falls in an area, it can weaken trees and increase the acidity of lakes and streams, making it difficult for fish to survive.

It's interesting to note, though, that all rainwater is acidic. Even clean rain picks up some carbon dioxide from the atmosphere to form carbonic acid (H_2CO_3). This is a very weak acid, but over long periods of time it alters the surface of the Earth. Rainwater seeps into the ground. It then breaks down rocks to form soil and eats away at limestone to make caves.

This solvency superpower comes from the way oxygen and hydrogen atoms arrange themselves in a water molecule. One side of the molecule, made up of the two hydrogen atoms, is positively charged, while the other side, made up of one oxygen atom, is negatively charged. So water attracts both positively and negatively charged molecules. As a result, water easily picks up chemicals, minerals, and nutrients as it flows through the Earth. A glass of water contains much more than just H_2O molecules. You're usually also chugging down some calcium, magnesium, and sodium. These tagalong elements are important for your health. However, water can also easily pick up poisons from pollution. Polluted water is usually more acidic than usual, making it hard for fish or other living things to survive in it.

Acids and Bases

Water ranges in acidity, which is measured with the **pH** scale. If you've ever taken care of a fish tank, you may have used a little strip of paper to make sure the pH of the water was safe for fish. If the pH is too high or too low, or changes too rapidly, fish can get sick or even die. You can add chemicals to the tank to help raise or lower the pH.

H ¹

Hydrogen

The letters pH actually stand for "potential of hydrogen." A water molecule, H_2O, may split into two ions, called H+ and OH−. When you measure water's pH, you're counting how many of each ion exists in the solution. Pure H_2O has an even balance of the two, so it's considered neutral. Acids, like vinegar or lemon juice, have low pH (meaning lots of H+). They also taste sour. Bases, such as baking soda or ammonia, have high pH (meaning lots of OH−) and taste bitter. But don't think that a taste test for pH is a good idea. Compounds at the high and low ends of the pH scale are very dangerous. They can burn your skin or corrode metal.

The hydrogen ion H+ is an important component of all acids, from tomato juice (which contains ascorbic acid, also known as vitamin C) to battery acid (sulfuric acid). Your stomach contains hydrochloric acid, which helps kill bacteria and digest food. Adding a metal to an acid triggers a chemical reaction that releases hydrogen gas and leaves behind a substance called a salt. This is the same type of reaction that revealed hydrogen to early chemists.

Human digestion

Black Gold

What do motor oil, gasoline, and plastic have in common? They all contain hydrogen combined with carbon into molecules called **hydrocarbons**. Carbon and hydrogen can combine together into

 Hydrogen Peroxide

When you get a cut or scrape, it needs to be cleaned out. Many people keep a bottle of hydrogen peroxide on hand for this purpose. The stuff stings like crazy, but it does the trick. As the 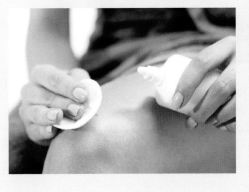 name suggests, hydrogen peroxide is a combination of hydrogen and oxygen with the chemical formula H_2O_2. The bottle in your medicine cabinet, though, is a mixture that contains mostly water. At concentrations of higher than eight percent hydrogen peroxide, the chemical burns human skin. Higher concentrations can be useful, though, for bleaching cotton, textiles, or wood pulp.

H 1

Hydrogen

Natural gas is a compound that includes hydrogen.

chains of varying length and complexity. The gas methane (CH_4) is the main ingredient in natural gas, a common fuel for heating and producing electricity. One molecule of methane contains one carbon atom surrounded by four hydrogen atoms. A molecule of the gas propane, commonly used in camp stoves, contains three carbon atoms joined with eight hydrogen atoms. In contrast, paraffin wax, a hard, white substance often used in candles, is composed of large molecules that each contain around 20 to 30 carbon atoms surrounded by more than twice as many hydrogen atoms.

Hydrocarbons formed naturally deep inside the Earth. Ancient, microscopic sea creatures died and sank to the bottom of the ocean. Their bodies were buried under layers of sand and rock. Over millions of years, heat and pressure transformed their remains into crude oil and natural gas. People can drill down into the earth to extract these hydrocarbons for use as fuels and other products. Oil is so important to our world economy that it's often referred to as "black gold." The crude oil that comes up out of the earth, though, is not quite ready to be used. It contains a mix of many different hydrocarbons. Refineries separate the crude oil into a variety of different products, from the gasoline we pump into our cars to the tar we spread on our highways.

 Text-Dependent Questions

1. What might a glass of water contain in addition to H_2O molecules?

2. Why would taking care of a fish tank help you learn about the pH scale?

3. How did hydrocarbons such as crude oil and natural gas form?

Research Project

How did water arrive on Earth? All the water in our oceans, rivers, and lakes wasn't here when the planet formed. Look up two scientific theories for how water got here and explain them both in your own words.

H ¹

Hydrogen

WORDS TO UNDERSTAND

ammonia   a colorless gas with a pungent odor

biomass gasification   a process that converts organic materials into the gases carbon monoxide, hydrogen, and carbon dioxide

electrolysis   a chemical change caused by sending an electrical current through a solution

electrolyte   a substance (such as the liquid in a battery) that electricity can pass through

fuel cell   a battery-like device that uses a chemical reaction to produce electricity

methane   a colorless, odorless, flammable gas that is the main component of natural gas

plasma   a fourth state of matter in which electrons separate from atoms to form an ionized gas

steam reforming   a method to produce hydrogen and other gases from a hydrocarbon fuel such as natural gas

Hydrogen in Our World

n outer space, hydrogen is king. It keeps the stars shining by fueling the fusion reactions in their cores. Though it's normally invisible, hydrogen also paints nebulas with beautiful color. A nebula is a gigantic cloud of gas and dust. When energetic light from nearby stars hits hydrogen atoms in the gas, they give off hydrogen-alpha radiation, which appears as a magenta or red glow.

Even black, open space isn't completely empty. Molecules of gas and dust float here and there throughout the space between the stars. These bits of lonely, free-floating matter form the interstellar medium, which is about 90 percent hydrogen and nine percent helium. (The other one percent is most likely dust particles made of carbon and silicon.)

Hydrogen

Though hydrogen is the most common element in the universe, it only comes in third on Earth. Why? Hydrogen gas is so light that Earth's atmosphere can't hold onto all of it. The gas easily escapes into outer space. Instead, the hydrogen on Earth is almost all found *within* other molecules, such as water or hydrocarbons.

Hydrogen is a key ingredient of numerous oils used in creating a wide range of food products.

Yet hydrogen is extremely important to Earth's economy. Many industries rely on hydrogen as part of the manufacturing process. For example, the food industry makes hydrogenated oils. Hydrogen gas is an important ingredient in the chemical reaction that produces **ammonia**, a chemical used to make fertilizers that help farmers grow crops. Hydrogen is also an important part of the process of refining crude oil into fuels people can use, such as gasoline and diesel fuel. Hydrogen itself can also fuel cars, trucks, and

Hydrogen is part of fossil fuels, but can also be a fuel all by itself.

rocket ships. And these are only a few examples of hydrogen in our world. So where does all this hydrogen come from?

Splitting Molecules

People have come up with several ways to coax hydrogen atoms out of other molecules. The method that accounts for 95 percent of the hydrogen production in the United States is called **steam reforming**. Basically, steam reforming reshuffles the elements inside steam (H_2O) and methane (CH_4) using two successive chemical reactions. First, hydrogen gets separated out and carbon and oxygen end up stuck together as carbon monoxide (CO). Then, carbon monoxide is reacted with water to produce more hydrogen and carbon dioxide (CO_2).

Another method, **electrolysis**, involves zapping water with electricity. This process breaks H_2O apart into hydrogen and oxygen. It

takes a lot of power to split an H_2O molecule. As a result, electrolysis is almost twice as expensive as steam reforming. But some scientists are looking into better ways to split water, taking their inspiration from photosynthesis—the process plants use to convert energy from the sun into sugars they need to grow. As part of this process, plants split water molecules apart. So far, methods that re-create this process are too expensive or not efficient enough to take the place of steam reforming.

This factory takes farm and animal waste and turns it into biomass fuel.

Rotting plants and other solid waste can also generate hydrogen through a process called **biomass gasification**. The process is very similar to steam reforming, but it works with any carbon- and hydrogen-based feedstock. Basically, this process uses extremely high temperatures and steam to get hydrogen out of any organic material. The waste from people's trash cans contains mainly organic materials, such as paper, food scraps, and yard waste. Gasification can transform this garbage into useful gases. Agricultural waste works, too—such as the leftover parts of wheat or corn that aren't edible.

Bacteria can also help transform biomass into hydrogen through a process called fermentation. Some bacteria take in sugars and produce hydrogen and other chemicals. Using genetics, scientists could create new versions of these bacteria that maximize the amount of hydrogen produced.

Biomass gasification and fermentation both cost more than electrolysis or steam reforming and aren't as efficient. But the upside is that these methods could turn trash into treasure. Garbage dumps and harvested fields could someday provide a wealth of hydrogen gas.

From Hydrocracking to Crackers

Right now, hydrogen gas is mainly used in factories to help produce many different kinds of products. The most important products that depend on hydrogen gas are fertilizer and petroleum products.

H ¹

Hydrogen

 The Magic of Cow Poop

Organic farmers regularly pay money for poop. Cow poop, bird *guano*, and other animal manures provide nutrients that plants need to grow. The most important nutrient for plant growth is the element nitrogen, and manure is full of the stuff. Before the 20th century, farmers who needed nitrogen for their crops only had a few options: find some poop or compost, or grow beans (which help replenish nitrogen). Then the German chemist Fritz Haber changed everything.

Haber figured out how to pull nitrogen out of thin air. This chem-

ical reaction, called the Haber process, relies on hydrogen. It's a complicated process, but basically you just need to heat up nitrogen gas (which makes up 78 percent of regular air), add hydrogen gas, and increase the pressure. A final ingredient, known as a catalyst, triggers the reaction. Iron mixed with a little potassium works best.

The Haber process produces ammonia (NH_3), a gas with a pungent scent. Some people use products containing ammonia dissolved in water to clean floors or windows. But ammonia has an even more important use: fertilizer. Thanks to the Haber process, factories could start producing cheap, artificial fertilizers. Farmers could now buy these products to spread on their fields instead of poop. As a result, farmers could start cultivating larger and larger fields. Agriculture boomed. Thanks to Haber's insight, farms could suddenly feed a much larger human population. "We can still thank [Haber] for feeding most of the world's 6.7 billion people today," writes Sam Kean in the book *The Disappearing Spoon*.

Though it's nitrogen Haber was after, hydrogen is essential to the process. In fact, two thirds of the hydrogen gas produced in the world today goes towards the production of ammonia, and 90 percent of that ammonia is used in fertilizers.

After crude oil gets extracted from the earth, it has to be refined. The refining process produces a huge range of petroleum products, from gasoline and diesel fuel to paraffin wax and asphalt. Remember that these products are all made up of molecules called hydrocarbons, and each is a chain of carbon atoms surrounded by hydrogen. The longer the chain, the heavier and more solid the substance.

A technique called hydrocracking uses hydrogen gas, plus high

This jet was cleared for takeoff after hydrocracking produced its fuel.

temperature and pressure, to split very long chains apart. This turns heavy oil into lighter fuels such as diesel and jet fuel. Not all refineries use hydrocracking, but the technique is becoming more common. Hydrogen can also help clean sulfur contamination out of petroleum products. This helps to reduce the amount of pollution produced when the fuel is burned.

Many other industries also use hydrogen. Factories that produce steel and other metal alloys often use hydrogen mixed with other gases to prevent the metal from corroding. In electronics manufacturing—such as computers, video screens, and cell phones—hydrogen often plays a role as a carrier gas. It acts like a vessel to help bring other elements or compounds into the manufacturing process. Hydrogen is also used in chemical reactions to produce vitamins and other drugs. Some large power plants use hydrogen as a coolant to protect vital machinery from overheating. The food industry adds hydrogen to unsaturated fats to produce margarine or solid fat for products such as crackers and cookies, though this practice is becoming less common. See the section on Hydrogen and You for more details on the role of hydrogen in the food we eat.

H ¹

Hydrogen

 Natural Gas

In a way, hydrogen already fuels our world, since all fossil fuels contain hydrogen. The simplest and lightest fossil fuel, natural gas, contains mostly **methane** (CH_4). Natural gas is mined from rocks deep underground, often using a controversial technique known as hydraulic fracturing, or "fracking" for short. Many homes and businesses use natural gas for heating or cooking. Natural gas power plants burn the fuel in order to generate electricity.

Many experts argue that natural gas is a cleaner option than other fossil fuels. While it is almost certainly a better alternative than coal, it still contributes to climate change. Methane is actually a more potent greenhouse gas than carbon dioxide, and methane may leak during natural gas extraction and transportation.

Like the hydrogen it contains, methane is also explosive. Natural gas leaks have led to explosions, such as the one at the *Deepwater Horizon* oil rig in April 2010 that caused one of the biggest oil spills in history.

Fuel of the Future

In the future, hydrogen may have an even more exciting application: It could power our world without directly contributing to climate change or pollution.

The sign says it all: Though highly useful, hydrogen is also highly dangerous.

Current fuels, such as gasoline, natural gas, coal, and oil, all release lots of CO_2 as well as some toxic gases when burned. When hydrogen burns, the only byproduct is water.

But hydrogen doesn't need to burn in order to produce electricity. A hydrogen **fuel cell** is like a battery that takes in hydrogen and produces electrical power through a chemical reaction. Like a battery, the fuel cell has a negative side and a positive side. A substance called an **electrolyte** acts like a gate that keeps the two sides separate and only allows certain ions to pass through.

As hydrogen fuel flows into the cell, a chemical called a catalyst strips electrons away from the atoms. The electrons form a current that flows out of the fuel cell. The hydrogen ions pass through the

Engineers are looking at hydrogen as one of several alternative fuels for cars.

electrolyte and combine with oxygen from the air to form water as a by-product. However, this amazing technology is hard to make cheap enough, reliable enough, and efficient enough.

Many different varieties of hydrogen fuel cells exist. They each use a different substance as the electrolyte. The choice of electrolyte can vary widely, from solid metals to super-hot molten salts. The type of electrolyte helps determine the specifics of the chemical reaction, the temperature at which the fuel cell operates, how expensive it is to make, and how efficient it is at producing electricity. In addition, some fuel cells require pure hydrogen fuel, while others can tolerate some contamination from other elements or compounds.

A fuel cell provided electricity and drinking water to astronauts aboard the Apollo spacecraft. In 2014, car companies introduced the first fuel cell vehicles to consumers in the United States. Fuel cell cars operate like other electric cars, but instead of plugging in to recharge, they fill up with hydrogen fuel.

One critique of hydrogen fuel cell technology, though, is that it doesn't actually get rid of our dependence on fossil fuels. In order to use a fuel cell, you need hydrogen. And the current best method to produce hydrogen requires natural gas. The second-best method, electrolysis, requires electricity that is usually produced by burning fossil fuels.

However, hydrogen technology could also pair nicely with renewable energy sources. A problem encountered with solar panels and wind turbines is that they only generate electricity when the sun is shining or the wind is blowing. At night or during a calm period, a backup source needs to generate power. One possible solution is to use excess electricity during very sunny or windy periods to perform electrolysis, which splits water into hydrogen and oxygen. Then, those

Hydrogen could be the key to capturing wind energy.

Hydrogen

gases can be stored. Later, the hydrogen and oxygen can feed back into a fuel cell to generate electricity again.

The Secrets of the Stars

Maybe someday we'll live in a world of solar panels, wind turbines, and fuel cell vehicles with hydrogen fueling stations on every block. But there's another possible future for hydrogen. If we learn the secrets of the stars, hydrogen could provide us with abundant amounts of cheap energy through nuclear fusion. Fusing atoms together releases almost four million times more energy than you get when you burn fossil fuels.

Inside of stars, including our own sun, gravity is incredibly strong. Hydrogen atoms get squashed together so tightly that they fuse into helium, releasing an incredible amount of energy in the process. Every second that goes by, the sun consumes about 600 million tons of hydrogen.

However, we can't reproduce the sun's gravity on Earth. Instead, scientists have come up with a different approach to make fusion work in our world. The reaction takes place in two of hydrogen's two

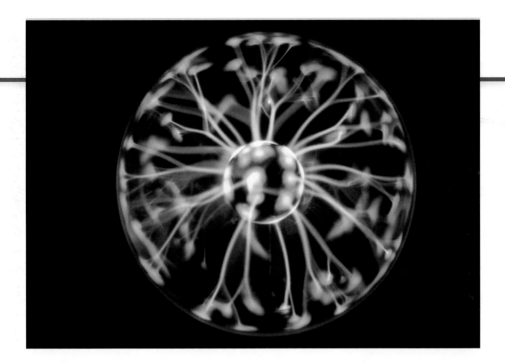

This lab device shows a type of matter known as plasma that is neither solid nor gas.

isotopes, deuterium and tritium. They fuse to form helium and one neutron. Instead of using intense gravity to force fusion, laboratories on Earth must convert deuterium and tritium to a state of matter called **plasma**, and keep that plasma contained at an extremely high temperature long enough for the atoms to crash into each other and combine.

Harnessing plasma isn't easy—physicist Richard Feynman once compared the task to trying to contain Jell-O with rubber bands. Scientists either use high-energy lasers or powerful magnets to keep plasma in check. The process of creating and maintaining plasma requires a lot of energy—so much that most fusion reactors on Earth

Hydrogen came from the stars and new supernovas are still blasting it out.

take in more energy than they generate. But scientists are making progress. A 2014 experiment showed that it was possible for a fusion reaction in a laboratory to create more energy than it used.

However, it will still take many more years of work before fusion technology is practical and cheap enough to provide energy on a large scale. "Fusion is an expensive science, because you're trying to build a sun in a bottle," said physicist Michael Williams of Princeton University in the *Huffington Post*.

Whether or not we succeed in creating bottled stars, hydrogen will remain one of the most important elements in our world and in the universe as a whole. Next time you feel the sun beating down, take a sip of water, or eat a peanut butter sandwich, think about how hydrogen made all these things possible.

 Text-Dependent Questions

1. What are three different methods of hydrogen production?

2. Why isn't hydrogen fuel cell technology already widespread?

3. Why does it make sense to call fusion technology a "sun in a bottle"?

Research Project

Choose an industry or product that uses hydrogen, such as fertilizer or oil refining. Research hydrogen's role in the process. How much hydrogen is used? Where does it come from? If it's involved in a chemical reaction, how does the reaction work? How important is hydrogen to that industry or product?

FIND OUT MORE

Books

Challoner, Jack. *The Elements: The New Guide to the Building Blocks of Our Universe.* London: Carlton Books, 2012.

Emsley, John. *Nature's Building Blocks: An A–Z Guide to the Elements.* Oxford: Oxford University Press, 2001.

Gray, Theodore. *Elements: A Visual Exploration of Every Known Atom in the Universe.* New York: Black Dog & Leventhal, 2012.

Newton, David E. *Chemical Elements, Vol. 2, G–O.* Detroit: Gale Cengage Learning, 2010.

Websites

www.rsc.org/periodic-table/podcast/1/hydrogen
The Royal Society of Chemistry has produced podcasts on all of the elements, including hydrogen. Listen here.

energy.gov/eere/fuelcells/hydrogen-production
An excellent graphic on this website illustrates the future of hydrogen production. The site also provides information on many other aspects of hydrogen and energy.

www.nrel.gov/hydrogen/
The National Renewable Energy Laboratory provides a wealth of information on hydrogen production and delivery, hydrogen storage, and fuel cell technology.

SERIES GLOSSARY OF KEY TERMS

carbohydrates a group of organic compounds including sugars, starches, and fiber

conductivity the ability of a substance for heat or electricity to pass through it

inert unable to bond with other matter

ion an atom with an electrical charge due to the loss or gain of an electron

isotope an atom of a specific element that has a different number of neutrons; it has the same atomic number but a different mass

nuclear fission process by which a nucleus is split into smaller parts, releasing massive amounts of energy

nuclear fusion process by which two atomic nuclei combine to form a heavier element while releasing energy

organic compound a chemical compound in which one or more atoms of carbon are linked to atoms of other elements (most commonly hydrogen, oxygen, or nitrogen)

solubility the ability of a substance to dissolve in a liquid

spectrum the range of electromagnetic radiation with respect to its wavelength or frequency; can sometimes be observed by characteristic colors or light

Hydrogen

INDEX

acid rain 38

Atomic Energy Commission 20

Big Bang 10

biomass gasification 48

Boyle, Robert 14, 15

carbohydrates 32, 33, 34

Cavendish, Henry 15, 16, 17

cow manure 50, 51

Deepwater Horizon 54

deuterium 25

Eiffel Tower 17

Fermi, Enrico 20, 21

France 13, 17

Greece 13

Haber, Fritz 50, 51

H-bomb 20

Hindenburg 19

hydrocarbons 41, 42, 43

hydrocracking 52, 53

hydrogen balloon 17, 18

hydrogen fuel cell 11, 55, 56

hydrogen, origin of 35, 36, 58

hydrogen and nutrition 30, 31, 32, 33

hydrogen, properties of 23 24

hydrogen, transporting 28, 29, 55

Jupiter 27

Lavoisier, Antoine 15, 16, 17

NASA 27, 28

natural gas 54

phlogiston 15, 16

"pop" test 24

Rabi, Isidor 20, 21

Soviet Union 30

Stahl, Georg Ernst 16

tritium 25

Urey, Harold C. 25

water 35, 36, 37

Williams, Michael 60

World War II 20

Zeppelins 17, 18, 19

Photo Credits

Adobe Images: Sved Oliver 12, Epicstockmedia 34, Nikkytok 37, Hamik42, Coffeekai 46, Saengsuriya13 47, Kletr 48, AF 50, Jjava 57. Department of Defense: 21, 54 (Coast Guard). Dreamstime.com: Koya79 7, Satori 22, martinmark 33, VickiFrance 38, Robertprzybysz 41, Lars Christensen 52, Warren Rosenberg 56. NASA: 10, 44, 55, 60. Wikimedia: 14, 18, 59.

About the Author

Kathryn Hulick started writing about science after returning from two years teaching English in the Peace Corps in Kyrgyzstan. She now lives in Massachusetts with her husband and son. They like to hike, read, cook, visit the ocean, and play with their dog, Maya. Hulick has written numerous books and articles for children and young adults, about everything from outer space to video games. Learn more on her website: http://kathrynhulick.com.